Wood Turtles

A Pet Care Guide for Wood Turtles

Wood Turtles General Info, Purchasing, Care, Cost, Keeping, Health, Supplies, Food, Breeding and More Included!

By Lolly Brown

Foreword

Wood Turtles are a great pet choice if you want to start taking care of turtles. It is a friendly and popular turtle breed, has a sweet personality, well-behaved and easy to handle. These turtles are known for its active and alert personality.

They are also branded as the most responsive type of turtles known to man, even comparing it to dogs. Its shell is wonderfully sculpted, showing red to bright yellow/orange skin, which is pleasing to one's eyes. They also possess beautiful black eyespots with yellow and orange swirls that would amaze you. Also known as the "Ornate Wood Turtle, "these turtles are very common to the pet trade world. They are imported to and from Costa Rica.

This book will deal with everything you need to know about Wood Turtles. You'll get to know its colorful history, breeding information, health and welfare, and other essential information. We hope you enjoy this fun-filled journey in buying and raising your very own Wood Turtle!

Table of Contents

Introduction...1

Chapter One: Wood Turtles 101..3

   Facts about Wood Turtles 4

   Size, Life Span, and Physical Appearance...........................5

      Quick Facts 6

Chapter Two: Wood Turtles as Pets 9

   What Makes It a Great Pet? 10

   Choosing Your Wood Turtle 11

   Wood Turtles Licensing 13

   Conservation Connection 15

   Cost of Owning a   Wood Turtle....................................16

   Is Your Budget Ready? 16

Chapter Three: Purchasing a Wood Turtle...........................23

   Where to Purchase Your Wood Turtle...............................24

   The Reputable and Smart Wood Turtle Breeder............27

   Characteristics of a Healthy Breed....................................31

   List of Breeders and Rescue Websites...............................31

Chapter Four: Proper Housing for Your Wood Turtles 37

   Housing Requirements 38

      Cage..39

      UV & UVB Light..40

Night Light 42

Substrate 42

Humidifier 44

Terrarium 45

Heat Pads 45

Chapter Five: Diet for Your Wood Turtle 47

Nutrition in the Wild vs. In Captivity 48

Nutritional Needs in the Wild 48

Nutritional Needs in Captivity 49

Tips for Feeding Your Pet 50

Feeding Amount and Frequency 51

Juveniles 52

Adults 52

During Hibernation 52

The Best Turtle Food Brand for your Pet Wood Turtle .. 53

Chapter Six: Husbandry Requirements for Wood Turtles ... 57

A Happy and Healthy Home 58

Cage or a Terrarium 58

Temperature 59

Humidity 60

Filtration and Cleaning 60

Landscaping/Aquascaping 61

Lighting 62

Basic Housing Checklist: 63

Habitat Tips 63

Habitat Maintenance Tips 65

Chapter Seven: Handling and Hygiene of Your Wood
Turtles 67

Handling and the Hygiene of Your Pet 68

Grooming Your Pet Wood Turtle 70

Water Quality 71

Other Essential Information 73

Nails 74

Beaks 75

Chapter Eight: Breeding and Shipping Wood Turtles 77

Sexual Dimorphism 78

How to Set Up the Right Breeding Conditions 78

How to Breed Your Pet Wood Turtle 80

Egg Removal, Incubation and Hatching of Eggs 80

Raising Wood Turtles 82

Life Cycle of a Wood Turtle 82

How to Package Your Wood Turtles 85

Chapter Nine: Common Diseases and Treatments 89

Superficial Wounds 90

Respiratory Infection..91

Metabolic Bone Disease (MBD) 92

Diarrhea 93

Dehydration 93

Eye Problem 94

Abscesses 94

Shell Rot 95

Chapter Ten: Care Sheet and Summary.....................................97

Glossary..**111**

Photo Credits...117

References...119

Introduction

Wood Turtles are known for its ability to walk further than any other breed of turtles and can cope with the terrestrial and aquatic environments, easy to train, and relatively tame. These medium sized turtles are known for well-defined pattern found on top of their carapace, which looks like a set of pyramids.

Found on northern Costa Rica up to southern Nicaragua, these turtles made home on terrestrial or aquatic habitat, but when the temperature drops, they go back to large streams and rivers to hibernate and because the water will not freeze here.

In summer, these turtles like to walk along the shore to find food and hydrate itself. Wood Turtles are daytime animals and would like roam around and suck up all the sunlight it can get. They can set up home for around 2.5 to fifteen acres and well within short distance of water throughout the year.

They were first hunted as human food but were later on collected for pet trade due to its big decrease in population. These turtles as easy to feed as they are omnivorous and would easily eat slugs, tadpoles, insects, algae, wild fruit, grass, leaves, carrion, moss, and even worms.

You might think turtles are easy to take care and breed, but they are not! They still need special attention to satisfy its need. You still need to know how to raise it properly, give proper care and health protection, so it can have a happy and healthy lifestyle.

In this book, we will help you decide whether these wood turtles are the right pet for you. At the end of this book, you will gain new knowledge about them. Happy reading!

Chapter One: Wood Turtles 101

Wood turtles are a great turtle breed if you want to start taking care of turtles. They are intelligent, easy to train, as well as easy to feed. They have doglike characteristics that will ease you in taking care of it. These turtles live easily on both aquatic and terrestrial territories wherever it might need to live. In winder, they dig deep holes or stay in deep rivers and streams to prevent from freezing. First of all, these turtles might be a different path for you to take. But this path will lead you to utmost joy and peace. These turtles are quick to learn and easy to live with, you will not regret investing in these little species overtime.

Here, we will give you the essential information, such as the biological facts, its colorful history, and evolution of this turtle. This will arm you with the essential knowledge in taking care and learning about this species. This and all the other information that you will learn in the succeeding chapter will help you understand your desired pet – Wood Turtles.

Facts about Wood Turtles

Wood turtles belong to the family of Emydidae, which can be found in the North eastern part of the United States up to the Canadian territory. A number of these species and its family are well distributed in Mexico, Northern Ecuador, and Northern part of Brazil. They typically live in savannahs, on riverbanks, or in forests where they can love peacefully.

Some of these species are only found in Costa Rica and Nicaragua. Wood turtles are somehow endangered because of people keeping it as pets and inaccessibility.

These turtles go back and forth the riverbanks and terrestrial area. In early June, turtles move away from the stream up to 1,000 feet. They go to wetlands, woods, and meadows area.

Females with eggs go to nesting area in mid June. Some may even travel up to one mile to build a nest. From June to September, turtles spend time away from the stream but may go frequently go back to it for short period of times. Breeding occurs in streams and happens in August to November. Also, breeding does not occur during spring.

Turtles, then, stay underwater during the months of November to April. They absorb oxygen through their skins. They could move in the stream, but they usually stay in a secured and protected area.

Size, Life Span, and Physical Appearance

Adult wood turtles are around five to nine inches (14 to 20 centimeters) mainly depending on the place of origin, on some states, these turtles can have a length as long as 216mm.

Popularly, wood turtles are also known as "old red leg" due to its brick-red or orange leg color. Unlike other turtles, these turtles do not shed their shells but rather develop a gnarled, rugged appearance especially when they grow older. The unique characteristic of this specie is its pyramid shape on the upper part of the shell.

An adult turtle has black head with occasional light dots or any other similar markings. The upper legs' scales are black to brownish. Throat, lower neck, lower legs' skin can be yellow, orange, salmon-red or even orange-red with a mix of darker color.

During hatching, the shell could be gray or brown in color. An adult wood turtle reaches sexual maturity at the age of 14 to 18. When wood turtles are in the wild, it can live up to 40 years, but when in captivity, it lives up to 58 years.

Quick Facts

Distribution and Range: scattered around United States and Canada particularly in Maine, Delaware, New York, Maryland, Massachusetts, Michigan, Iowa, Vermont, New Brunswick, Connecticut, Quebec, Rhode Island, Pennsylvania, New Hampshire, Virginia, West Virginia, Rhode Island, Nova Scotia, and Ontario.

Breed Size: medium size

Body Type and Appearance: lower shell is yellow with big black blotches on each segment. The top and rear leg portions can be black, brown, or gray. There is a yellowish and orange shade on the skin between the scales, throat, and leg sockets.

Length: average of fourteen to 20 centimeters, some might go up to 211 millimeters. Male reaches up to 23.4 cm while female reaches up to 20.4 cm.

Height: seven to nine inches

Weight: an adult turtle could weigh as heavy as a kilo

Skin Texture: the texture is rough, sculpted shell

Color: Have a black and yellow pattern with dark patches and several yellowish spots. There are variations in the vibrancy of colors

Temperament: alert, inquisitive, responsive, "dog-like"

Diet: opportunistic eaters who are also omnivores; eats a variety of plant material such as various berries, leaves, and mushrooms, mollusks, young mice, amphibians, carrion, earthworms, insects

Habitat: prefers both terrestrial and aquatic habitat; needs small to fast moving streams, terrestrial habitat is required for nesting purposes. They tend to live in deciduous and coniferous forests.

Health Condition: gets along well with other pets

Behavior: In Spring, they are in vegetation. During the summer, they are on terrestrial grounds. During the winter, they stay under the water.

Life Span: 40 years in the wild, while 58 years in captivity

These are just some basic information that you need to know about your wood turtle. You need to know this information as you this wood turtle would stay with you for a very long time. If you are still determined to own your very first wood turtle, read on to know more about these lovely creature. Have fun reading!

Chapter Two: Wood Turtles as Pets

Now, you have the basic idea about what Wood Turtles are, further, you have possessed the knowledge on its history and quick facts. It is now time to determine whether this turtle is a great pet for you. We will dig deeper into this little specie by learning its behavioral traits, permits and licenses you need to keep them, an estimated budget so you can provide all of its need.

These are some things that you need to remember before you purchase your first Wood Turtle. They may be little creature, but taking care of it as a pet needs total commitment. Read on this chapter to gain more knowledge about your desired pet.

What Makes It a Great Pet?

Buying your first pet can be a difficult decision. You need to put your all heart and soul to this creature as you need to take care of it as if it your own child. If you are planning to start taking care of reptiles, wood turtles are a great way to begin with.

You might be scared to take care of reptiles, as they might behave differently than other pets that you know. Wood turtles, although endangered, can be easily found in the United States and Canada. They are known to possess dog like characteristics that would ease up any pet parent. They can be taught easily as they are alert and inquisitive creature.

Temperament and Behavioral Characteristics

- They tend to move from terrestrial and aquatic area.
- Male wood turtles are very aggressive.
- They capture their prey easily through stumping their feet imitating the sound of the rainfall.
- They are docile creatures.
- They are shy.
- If they are trained in a proper environment, they can become excellent pets.

- They spend time foraging for food.
- They bask.
- They rarely venture away from the place they were born, in its entire life.
- Intelligent
- It can live in streams, creeks, woods, thickets, meadows, rivers, and swamps.
- They hibernate in winter.
- They are quite agile.

These are some of the temperament and behavioral characteristics of your pet wood turtle. You could discover new characteristics as you bond and raise your own pet.

Choosing Your Wood Turtle

In this section, we will give you further information on why you should or you should not keep this turtle as your household pet. Take note of these things as they will give you extreme help in making your decision.

Pros

- Suited for those who want to own turtles for the first time.
- Easily available to purchase.
- They are docile and easy to train.
- They are safe around people as long as it is properly handled.
- They do not shed unlike other pets.
- They require little to no supervision at all.
- They only need a secure and safe enclosure with food and water.
- They can eat whatever you will give it because they are omnivorous animals and opportunistic eaters.
- They are easy to train, tamed, and can socialize well with other people.
- They can live up to fifty years.

Cons

- The price of these turtles might be higher than other pets you have owned.
- They live up to fifty years; you need to have long term commitment to provide its need.
- They are not as active as other pets.
- Your children may not like it because they can't play it unlike other pets.

If you still want to purchase the wood turtles even after going through the pros and cons, continue reading as you need to know more about them, the further costs and licenses that you need to get when you purchase them.

Wood Turtles Licensing

If you are planning to purchase Wood Turtles, you need to have it licensed so you can be protected and you need to follow these rules and regulation. Different countries, regions, and states have different licensing requirements, especially for reptiles.

There is a specific organization that is responsible in taking care of all animal species, especially the endangered kind, it is the Convention on International Trade in Endangered Species (CITES). CITE member countries are USA, Europe, Asia, Australia, and the Latin America. You need to prepare all the legal and proper documents regarding the animal that you want to keep as pet in case there are any troubles.

In CITES, there are specific appendices for different species in different categories. There are categories and different rules for exporting, keeping, and trading wood turtles. Turtles, wood turtles in particular, belong to CITES appendix II, which means they are specifically not threatened of extinction, but its trade should be control to avoid extinction or even using it beyond its capacity to survive.

You will not be able to travel with your Wood Turtle from one country to another one if you do not have the certificate of export coming from CITES (country of origin) as well as the certificate of import from CITES (country of destination). You need to bring the necessary certificates to present to the authorities to prove that you have bought your pet legally and you will be travelling it to and fro legally and safely.

You do not really need to ask for approval from any authorities or organizations. You just need to provide the necessary documents such as the name, identity, and the specifics of your wood turtle. It should also contain the name, address, contact details, and basic information where you bought your pet. Further, also provide your personal information in the document. These documents should be well kept for future reference.

Trade is controlled for animals under the Appendix II you need necessary permits, documents, and approval to trade or breed it locally and internationally. If you fail or you get caught trading, buying, or breeding illegally, CITES may have to confiscate your wood turtles and other paraphernalia.

Conservation Connection

Even if most wood turtle have a 'least concern' conservation status, these reptiles are still very important to the environment and the ecosystem as a whole because they fill a role in the food chain. Wood turtle, especially those living in the wild are also helpful in controlling agricultural pests like rodents and various types of insects. Aside from that they can also help in dispersing seeds in the wild.

What many breeders and wildlife experts are getting concerned about is the growing trend of using a turtle's skin as a material for the creation of shoes, bags, boots and other fashion products. In a 10 year period, 1,000 Wood Turtle skins were imported in America that was used in the production of such products. Many wildlife organizations don't recommend buying such products especially if you're in abroad to help stop these companies who are killing these reptiles.

Cost of Owning a Wood Turtle

The cost of owning a wood turtle includes many aspects. You need to take note of the following things such as: searching and buying the wood turtle, enclosure or tank or aquarium, water dishes, food bowls, supplies such as different bulbs for great heat sources, reptile humidifier, and food supplies. If you think you can handle these following expenses, you can go ahead and purchase your first wood turtle.

Is Your Budget Ready?

Taking care of a new pet is not easy. You need to plan out everything and you need to prepare yourself for this big responsibility that you will go through. Having a pet is like having your own child; you need to provide it with shelter, food, water, and other basic necessities. You need to set aside a budget to raise your own pet.

Setting aside a budget for your pet might be difficult at first, but it will be amazing when you get a hang of it. The total cost of your expenses will depend upon the type and kind of resources that you will buy. Some items might have higher prices due to limited stocks.

You also need to keep in mind the quality of your product and how long it will last. It might be cheaper but if you need to buy if more often – it is not worth it. This section will help you decide if you are ready to own your very first Wood Turtle.

Wood Turtle's Price

Wood Turtles vary greatly in prices. You need to be mindful of the kind of wood turtle that you want to purchase. An approximate cost of a wood turtle is around $395 to $595, well depending to age and structure.

If the turtle came from a very well-bred wood turtle hatching, it will cost you around $300 to $316. While a well-bred will cost you around $279 and the prettiest wood turtle would cost you around $396.

It might be expensive, but wood turtles are a good investment if you really want to try it. Find a respectable breeder or store so you can be assured that the hatchlings are well taken care of.

Other Turtle Essentials

Buying a wood turtle is a difficult process. You need to be financially prepared with all the other essentials that you need to purchase. You must keep in mind that some of these expenses are recurrent while some are just only bought once. You need to find the best brand and the best quantity so you can get the best value for your money.

Turtle Crate: $130 - $280

The first thing that you need to buy is a crate or a cage, especially if you do not have a big place for it to roam around or if you have kids and other pets present in the area. Kids should be kept away from turtles especially if you just introduce the pet to your kids. They might play with it just like a regular pet and the turtle might end up biting it. Also, the presence of other pets might scare off your turtle. Or worse, it might eat and kill it.

Crates come in various prices because of the quality and size. You can buy a big crate for your pet; this will ensure that your pet turtle will have a space to walk around. Further, you need to allot an allowance space for the turtle because it will grow and needs a big space. Further, this can be used as transport during veterinary consultation.

Aquarium Substrate: $17 - $25

An aquarium substrate is essential to keeping your wood turtle happy. They need to have both terrestrial and aquatic environment present around them, especially during the changing of the season. Aquarium substrate are used for cover at the bottom of their tank or habitat, there are a lot of choices on what aquarium substrate you can use.

This ready-made substrate is very convenient for busy owners. You just need buy a bunch then throw if off the tank, but sometimes, your wood turtle might get hurt or end up eating substrate by accident. Other choices that you can use are: live plants, which can also be used as food by your turtle.

You need to find other substrate that would create a natural environment such as:

o **Fine Sand** - This is a standard substrate especially for starting pet owners, but it is very difficult to clean through frequent vacuuming. If you choose this option, you need to buy clean, fine sand and clean it frequently or else your tank will become a mess.

o **Gravel** - If you are planning to set up a big aquarium, gravel is a good choice, especially if you intend to put gravel on the bottom of the substrate. But, if you are just getting a small aquarium, this is not advised.

o **Fluorite** - This could be a great choice if you plan to design your own substrate. It is a very good choice for plants, looks attractive and natural, and your turtle won't be attractive to eat it. Do not be scared if your water looks dirty at first, let the fluorite settle first.

UVB & UV Light: $10 - $50

Reptiles have four color receptors, green, red, blue, and the fourth, that allows them to see UVA light. This light is allowing them to see patterns and colors which humans cannot. This UV light can allow them to recognize another animal from the same species and also detect if there is any movement in the area. Also, this will help them stimulate appetite through making the food more appealing and yummy. UVA light presence promotes reproduction, basking, social behavior, proper foraging, activity level, feeding, and digestion.

UVB light, on the other hand, is essential for the production of Vitamin D3 and calcium for your reptile. When your pet is exposed with UVB light, this will synthesize the production of Vitamin D3 into one's skin. This vitamin D3 helps the reptile absorb and use calcium. Further, vitamin D3 is used for the following: immune system regulation helps in organ development promotion, and mineral metabolism just like calcium.

On the other hand, if you fail to provide Vitamin D3 to your pet, it will suffer from sickness such as hypocalcaemia or the chronic calcium deficiency, metabolic bone disease, which can also cause bone deformities and will be fatal if not treated properly.

Night Light Bulbs: $7 - $10

Aside from having UV & UVB light, you need to provide night light bulbs. You need to provide the biggest turtle tank as possible for your pet because you need to provide areas with different temperature or a thermal gradient. This gradient is essential to contribute good health and will allow the reptiles to have a regulated body temperature through moving through hot and cool area.

Reptile Humidifier: $60 - $80

Reptiles still need moisture even through the dry seasons; this is the reason why you need to provide reptile humidifier to provide a misty environment on its substrate. These are all the things that you need if you want to raise your own pet wood turtle. Make sure that you have these ready before you bring your pet wood turtle at home. If you have purchase your pet before setting up its home, you might get into trouble and your pet might have a difficult time in adjusting and adapting into a new and fresh environment.

Chapter Three: Purchasing a Wood Turtle

Here, we will provide you with great criteria on how to select a great breed of Wood Turtle and also critique how to spot a trustworthy and reputable breeder. We will also give you tips on how to purchase your wood turtle legally. You need to know the background of your pet before purchasing it, its breeding and who raise it. Also, we will provide you with sites where you can purchase wood turtle legally and can help you decide on the best wood turtle deal that you can get. You need to keep in mind that buying a great breed is an essential thing to do if you want to keep a healthy breed.

A well-bred wood turtle would give you a breeze in taking care of it. Be aware of the warning signs that might tell you that the breed that you will choose is not perfect for you.

Where to Purchase Your Wood Turtle

In this part, we will be giving you place where you can purchase your own wood turtle and how to spot if the seller is selling it legally or illegally. There are a lot of choices in this section, thus, we will be providing you with the pros and cons so you can choose the best choice possible.

Keep an open mind with all of these choices easily available to you, find on that are easily convenient to you and would present you with the best result possible. But, you can also ask around and seek advice from professionals and friends.

Nearby Pet Stores or Pet Farms

Local pet stores are the first choice if you do not have much time to search and screen places to buy your first pet. You just head off to the nearest pet store and buy yourself your wood turtle.

Advantages:

- It is easily accessible to many areas.
- This option is great for those people who have little to no time in looking for the pet.

Disadvantages:

- Some stores might not have wood turtle.
- You could not know the background information of the breed that you would be buying.
- You need, still, to drive to the place where you can buy the pet.

Be mindful of the local pet store that you will go to. Some local pet stores are just 'production' companies that would produce their eggs in batches to make sure that they earn money.

Private Turtle Breeders

If you have already bought a pet before, this option might be good for you:

Advantages:

- You can know the background information of the wood turtle and its family.

- You can socialize with other owners and know how to take care of the pet yourself.
- You can bargain the price of the turtle.
- You can be assured that your wood turtle is well-taken care of.

Disadvantages:

- You need to find the best breeder possible, you do not settle with the first one that you find.
- You need to allot time in driving up to different locations.
- You might get scammed if you do not know how to ask the right questions.

Online Pet Shops, Online Sellers or Breeders Selling Through the Internet

The internet has given us a lot of chance to explore and find things we have not seen before. A good thing that the internet has given us are online stores, basically, they are sites that would provide you with great deals in buying pets.

Advantages:

- You just need to browse different websites to find the best deal possible.

- You can search everywhere! In between your breaks, before you sleep, before you go to work, basically – everywhere.
- You can have it delivered to you; you do not have to drive up to the location to purchase your pet.

Disadvantages:

- You can't really scrutinize the breed that they will give you.
- You might get scammed if you do not know how to ask the right questions.

The Reputable and Smart Wood Turtle Breeder

Selecting the person who you buy the turtles to is the first step in this process. You need to find a responsible, caring, and reputable breeder that you trust has raised the wood turtle well. A key to finding great breeders is asking the right questions about the breed that they rest, they need to give you the right answers about the breed that they have.

You need to find the breeder that had raised the wood turtle due to health purposes and not just for money. If the breeder only gives you basic information that you can get anywhere, s/he is definitely not a breeder.

Further, the chosen breeder must give you essential information such as housekeeping, humidity, food supply and etc. that is relevant in raising your pet. Respectable breeders often form networks to find new clients, try to ask around for suggestions.

This section will provide you with tips in finding the best Wood Turtle breeder:

- Ask your family, relatives, and friends if they know a caring and respectable breeder, this might be your key to finding the best one possible.

- Search and join online forums and talk to other pet enthusiasts and ask for suggestions where you can buy the pet.

- Find websites on Wood Turtles, more often than not, they link to reputable breeders.

- If the website doesn't provide any information about the facilities or the breeder, you shouldn't waste your time with them.

- Make sure these websites are real and have reputable background, check signs for bogusness, if you see a little red flag, back out now.

- Remove breeders who don't answer your questions truthfully and honestly, this will enable you if the breeders are actually reputable or just hobby breeders.

- Contact each breeder individually. Ask them of their knowledge and experience in breeding Shih Tzu.

- Expect a reputable breeder to ask you questions about yourself as well. A responsible breeder wants to make sure that his pups go to good homes.

- Make sure you allot time to go through every detail, although tedious, will give you amazing results.

- Schedule visits from your selected breeders; ask for a tour on their facilities.

- Narrow down, again, your choices. Remove those with unorganized and dirty facilities – you don't know if your future pup has been bred in this.

- If you still can't decide, go back to square one and list down every detail possible.

Some Questions You Can Ask to Spot a Good Breeder

- Can you tell me information about Wood Turtle or this particular breed?

- How many times should I feed it? How often? What food or brands can you recommend?

- What are the things I need for its habitat? Any stores or brands you can refer? What kind of enclosure does it prefer?

- How did you breed the wood turtle? How did you raise them?

- How do I set up its habitat? What should be the temperature?

- How many years have you been in business, and what kind of experience do you have as a breeder?

- What do you specialize in? What types of species do you breed and sell?

- Do you offer any kind of a warranty or guarantee? If so, how long?

- Can I ask any referrals?

Characteristics of a Healthy Breed

Whether you are planning to buy a baby or adult wood turtle, you need to keep in mind several characteristics in having the best breed possible.

First, you need to look at its eyes. Make sure that the eyes are free from any discharge or any other cloudiness. Also, you need to look at its breeding, make sure that there is no difficulty in breathing and no discharge from the nose. You should ask the breeder for any other specific information that you might want to know. Also, the wood turtle must be mobile and can move at its will.

Never acquire a wood turtle if it has suspicious markings or signs of health issues. Inspect the shell and body and make sure there is no parasite infection.

List of Breeders and Rescue Websites

We have provided you with a lot of ways on how to purchase your first wood turtle. You might want to give these sites a try if you do not have the luxury of time to go to different places or sites.

Aside from the hassle free searching, these sites could help you with the essential information about your pet. You can ask around and ask for suggestion on how to raise your wood turtles properly. These groups are quite knowledgeable about reptiles, in general, and wood turtles and might give you good advice on where to buy.

Here is the list of breeders and adoption rescue websites around United States and United Kingdom:

United States Breeders and Rescue Websites

The Turtle Source
<http://www.theturtlesource.com/i.asp?id=100200307>

Snakes at Sunset
<http://snakesatsunset.com/north-american-wood-turtle/>

Back Water Reptiles
<http://www.backwaterreptiles.com/turtles/central-american-ornate-wood-turtle-for-sale.html>

Tortoise Town
<https://www.tortoisetown.com/product/north-american-wood-turtle-for-sale/>

Garden State Tortoise

<http://www.gardenstatetortoise.com/north-american-wood-turtle>

CB Reptile

<https://www.cbreptile.com/painted-turtles-for-sale/>

Turtles and Tortoise Inc.

<http://www.turtlesandtortoises.com/North-American-Wood-Turtle-Caresheet.html>

Underground Reptiles

<https://undergroundreptiles.com/shop/baby-north-american-wood-turtle/>

Reptile City

<http://www.reptilecity.com/Merchant2/merchant.mvc?Screen=PROD&Product_Code=COWT&Category_Code=TURTLES>

Tortoise Forum

<https://tortoiseforum.org/threads/cb-north-american-wood-turtles.66322/>

Reptiles N Critters

<http://www.reptilesncritters.com/central-american-ornate-wood-tortoise.html>

United Kingdom Breeders and Rescue Websites

The Reptile Forum UK

<http://www.reptileforums.co.uk/forums/shelled-turtles-tortoise/594125-ornate-wood-turtles.html>

Exotic Pets

<https://www.exotic-pets.co.uk/turtles-for-sale.html>

Pets 4 Home

<https://www.pets4homes.co.uk/sale/reptiles/turtle//>

Peregrine Livefood

<http://peregrine-livefoods.co.uk/mexican-painted-wood-turtle//>

Shelled Warriors

<http://www.shelledwarriors.co.uk/forum/showthread.php?t=74148/>

These are some of the websites that you can access to gain new information and potential adopt and purchase your pet wood turtle. Make sure you go through this website as they also give you new information about them. Take time and read through them. As for the choices we have given you, you should be the one to get the best choice possible for you. What works for us might not work for you. Happy shopping!

Chapter Four: Proper Housing for Your Wood Turtles

By now, you have decided where to buy your wood turtle, and, probably have read relevant information about them. Further, you might possess new skill through communicating with your friends, family, and other breeders. After all these tasks, your job is not yet done.

You must now think of the habitat requirements and caging needs for your pet. This comes first before you think of the food, handling, and even breeding them. You must set-up the right environment like its housing need, materials to use, and other tips you need to have so your pet could have a happy lifestyle. This will prevent them from being stressed out.

These things are very essential and you need to buy these before you take home your very first wood turtle. If you fail to provide these things at first, you might have a hard time in taking care of your pet easily. There are many places you can buy these supplies. So buy them now before your time runs out. In this chapter, we will help you give the best for your pet. You will gain new knowledge from this portion so take note of these things very carefully.

Housing Requirements

Wood turtles are reptiles. This means they need different location and temperature to suffice their needs. Take note of these things as they are essential so your pet could have a happy and healthy lifestyle:

- Cage
- Light

- Night Light
- Substrate
- Humidifier
- Terrarium

These are some of the essential things that you need to buy. They might seem expensive at first, but it will be used for a long period of time. Buy the best brand as possible, as you will use this for your pet wood turtle for a very long time.

Cage

Wood turtles could reach up to eight inches in height and are pretty active most of the time. You need to provide a big space for it to move and walk around – which they need for them to have a good health and optimum wellbeing.

New hatchlings can be raised in aquariums, but adults need custom-built enclosures that contain a shallow water pool and substrate so it can play and be comfortable with the new environment. You do not really need to buy aquariums, you can also work with tubs, plastic containers o the like. You need a transparent casing so you can easily see your pet turtle while inside the tank.

You can DIY your own cage or terrarium if you are handy. This could be a great household activity with you and your friends. Also, this could be a great way to express your love for your pet.

UV & UVB Light

For turtles, light is very important. They just do not use light to see, the turtle's life depend on the light that you will give it.

A word of caution, you should not look directly at these lights, because these lights are very bright and could potentially hurt your eyes – or even worse, they could blind you if you stare at them long enough. Further, secure these lights in your turtle tank so it will not fall into the water. If these lights would fall into the water, your turtle could get electrocuted and possibly die. Make sure that you know how to properly wire your pet turtle's lights, if not, seek assistance from your friends and family.

There are three types of lights that you need to provide for your pet: natural sunlight, Ultraviolet A (UVA), and Ultraviolet B (UVB). These three are vital to provide a healthy lifestyle for your pet.

The UVB light is important to your reptile because it produces Vitamin D3. This is important for the production and usage of calcium and other important nutrients. If they are deprived of this vitamin, this would cause them metabolic bone disease and will eventually die. Make sure you buy and replace this lamp every six months – so set aside a budget for this need.

You also need to provide a basking lamp, daylight lamp that produces heat as well as light. This is important to maintain the temperature of the crate it has.

UVA, on the other hand, is needed for regulate one's mood, activity level, breeding and mating. As we have mentioned before, wood turtles can see much more color and light unlike humans or other pets; therefore, this light is important for them to properly experience and see the world around them. Further, this helps them identify wood turtles from the same species.

These lights are essential as your pet will not have an easy access on these things especially when you place it at home.

Night Light

Aside from buying the typical lights you also need to purchase night lights as this are important for your pets. These lights, which are either purplish-blue or red, allow the turtles to see around the night without emitting too much light. This night light also provides heat which is needed for hatchling turtles. Turtles would not mind what color is their night light – as long as it is not too light and will help them see during the night.

Substrate

Substrates are important because this serves as the 'ground' where the turtles could step on when it is place in the tank or the aquarium. You need to know the best kind of substrate that you will provide for your turtle. Here are some examples that you can choose from:

No Substrate Type of Enclosure

This is the easiest option that you can go with. You can easily clean your tank if it has no substrate on it, also, your turtle could be safe from eating the substrate.

Unfortunately, if you do not have a substrate, one can easily see how dirty your tank could be because turtles are naturally messy. Also, this could cause stress with your pet because it has nothing to burrow in. You can add plastic plants, but a danger for that choice is that your pet turtle might eat it.

Sand

A popular form of substrate is sand. Although it is difficult to clean with a siphon, it is very attractive to look at, also, it is not a health risk for your pet turtle. Further, your pet could burrow itself easily. But, remember, sand and filter does not mix; you may need to replace the motor of your filter often if you choose this choice.

Fine Gravel

This is an excellent choice if you want to create your own substrate. It is easy to clean, goes well with live plants, and easy for your turtle to burrow itself in. Unfortunately, this gravel is difficult to siphon, as some small gravel might get stuck in it.

Standard Gravel

These gravels are a popular choice and very common in most pet stores. These are natural looking and very attractive. Another bonus is that you can easily clean it with a siphon. Unfortunately, if your turtle is just small, it might experience difficulty in burrowing in.

River Rock

These rocks are as the size of a golf ball. They are good to look at and have no health risks. Unfortunately, these are very difficult to clean with a siphon. But, you can easily see this everywhere, and for a cheap price.

These are just some of the choices you can choose from to form your own substrate. Choose wisely as this will determine how healthy your wood turtle would be.

Humidifier

Wood turtles need humidifier especially during dry season. They need daily mist to keep them refreshed through different seasons.

Terrarium

This may be the biggest thing you need to accomplish when you want to have a great turtle habitat. Terrariums should be big enough to accommodate different regions – a wet region and a dry region. This could help your wood turtle be comfortable with its new environment.

Heat Pads

Heat pads are important to produce warmth for your pet. You just need to stick it at farthest end of the enclosure and let it do the rest. You need to constantly check the temperature as this might cause a raise of temperature that may be too hot for your wood turtle. But, this pad could lessen the cost of buying too much light.

These are just some of the things that you need to provide for your wood turtle. You need to purchase these items as they are vital to keep your pet happy and healthy. If you fail to provide one of these, this might compromise your pet's health.

Chapter Five: Diet for Your Wood Turtle

Having good nutrition is the key in having a happy and healthy pet. You need to get to know your pet before letting it anything. If you fail to provide the correct food for your pet, this might compromise its health and might even end up in death. Take note of these things as they are very important. In this chapter, we will provide you with the nutritional fact sheet for your pet. We also included some feeing tips, amount and frequency for your turtle to have a well-balanced and happy diet.

Nutrition in the Wild vs. In Captivity

Your wood turtle is an opportunistic and omnivorous feeder. It feeds whether in water or in land. An omnivore is an animal that can consume both plant and animal matter.

Further, it can consume leaves, fruit, or flower. You can even give it herbaceous and wooden plants, such as willows, dandelions, raspberries, strawberries, and violets. Also, it can consume grasses, snails, slugs, insects, earthworms, eggs, fungi, and carrion.

Nutritional Needs in the Wild

When your wood turtle is in the wild, it consumes different food. As we have mentioned before, wood turtles like eating earthworm. It is well noted that they also eat slugs, leeches, snails, and larvae. Sometimes they eat relatively large animals like frogs, newborn mice, and tadpoles.

They are both herbivores and omnivores. They can certainly eat algae and grasses as well. Further, they are seen to be eating leaves of willow, birch, alder and even cranberry leaves. They are also often seen eating cinquefoil, dandelions, and wild flowers. Some even see them eating corn off the cob! They eat the left overs of black bear and beavers.

Nutritional Needs in Captivity

When you have already purchased your pet, you can give these following foods to your wood turtle:

- Strawberries
- Raspberries
- Apple
- Bananas
- Cherries
- Pear
- Grapes
- Watermelon
- Cantaloupe
- Honeydew melon
- Carrots
- Mixed vegetables (purchased at supermarket)
- Spinach
- Romaine lettuce
- Corn
- Minnows
- Canned dog food
- Earthworms
- Adult live crickets
- Kitten chow
- Hard boiled egg
- Dead mice
- Chicken heart and liver

Tips for Feeding Your Pet

Feeding your pet could be a difficult task; you may not know how much is too much for it. Wood turtles will not give you obvious signs that it wants food. Rather, you need to allot time and effort to learn the feeding habits of your pet or better create a definite feeding habit for it to follow. If you have trained it enough, your wood turtle would have the cue when it needs to eat and when it wants to eat.

Here are some guidelines when you are feeding your pet wood turtle:

- Do not give them dairy products such as cheese, milk, and yoghurt. They can't digest dairy and will just cause illness.

- Give them fresh food but do not leave food on the cage as it may rot and create an unpleasant environment.

- Always clean your food dish before you give new food.

- Provide food in small portions, so it will be easier for your pet to eat and digest. They do not have teeth and only use jaws to cut their food.

- Provide great sources of protein every two to three days only and avoid giving too much.

- Do not give raw meat such as hamburger that could possibly rot.

These are some of the things that you need to remember when you are feeding your pet, especially when you are a novice pet owner. Take note of the things that your pet can and could not eat – it might cause allergic reactions that could even lead to death.

In this section, we will give you an insight on how to feed your pet wood turtle. All pets eat differently, you remember how much and how often your pet needs to eat.

Feeding Amount and Frequency

Wood turtles are very different from your typical pet. Unlike other pets, wood turtles do not need to be fed daily, but their requirements and frequency depends on several factors such as age and season.

Juveniles

In this stage, wood turtles need to be fed frequently. They need to receive calcium and vitamins around three times a week and needs to eat daily. Juveniles like to walk and roam around during morning and afternoon and they could be fed during this time.

Wood turtles are still considered as juveniles until they reach the age of 7. However, if your turtle, which is over three years old, is starting to eat less you can reduce feeding. You should consult a veterinarian to provide great health care for your pet.

Adults

Adult wood turtle could be fed every other day or even every other third day. Make sure you remove all the uneaten food after twenty minutes, unless it is live like crickets, earthworms, fish, or else it will cause an unpleasant odor and set an unhealthy environment for your pet.

During Hibernation

During hibernation, your pet wood turtle would sleep through winter. In this scenario, you should not feed your pet wood turtle anymore. Stop feeding it from fall but still provide him water for bathing.

The Best Turtle Food Brand for your Pet Wood Turtle

Feeding your pet could be a difficult task; you may not know how much is too much for it. Wood turtles will not give you obvious signs that it wants food. Rather, you need to allot time and effort to learn the feeding habits of your pet, or better, create a definite feeding habit for it to follow. If you have trained it enough, your wood turtle would have the cue when it needs to eat and when it wants to eat.

In this subsection, we will provide you with the top five turtle pet food that your pet wood turtle could enjoy. You are not limited to these choices as you can choose other brands, especially if it is recommended by your veterinarian. Also, you can ask other pet owners on what food they eat and the store where they buy it. Take caution as this is vital that could determine the overall health of your pet.

Here are our top five picks for your pet wood turtle's food:

Recommended Brand No. 1: Tetra ReptoMin Floating Food

This brand is reputable to several pet owners. This trusted brand for almost thirty years, provides a balanced and complete meal that your turtle will like, further, this formula is very easy to digest.

The food is kept in a Ziploc bag that would easy to reseal for convenient storage.

Recommended Brand No. 2: Rep-Cal Aquatic Turtle Food

A plus factor for this product – it ships internationally! This turtle food is filled with a lot of vitamins and minerals needed by your pet. It has a great deal of calcium and Vitamin D3 which are essential for your pet wood turtle's growth!

This food brand contains high quality of apple fiber and animal proteins. This product provides complete and balanced nutrition.

Recommended Brand No. 3: Zoo Med Natural Aquatic Turtle Food

What makes this pet food stand out from the other is that it is available in three sizes of pellets! One for your hatchling, another one is great for growth, and lastly, a formula for maintenance.

These pellet sizes and formulas are scientifically done to qualify and get all the dietary requirements for your pet. For the hatchling pellets, they have specifically designed their pellets to accommodate for growth and nutrition.

Recommended Brand No. 4: Mazuri Aquatic Turtle Diet

This turtle food brand is chosen by many pet owners. Some would even say that a bag of this product would last them for months! Think of the savings that you will have when you buy this product.

What makes this amazing is that this is great for all stages of development. You could give it to your hatchling or even an older pet. They product a holistic nutrition essential to every step or stage your pet will undergo.

Recommended Brand No. 5: Fluker's Aquatic Turtle Diet

Another great pet food that ships internationally, this pet food is what your pet is looking for!

Available in three sizes: 2 pack of eight ounces, four ounce pack, or eight ounce pack, this pet food is made from premium protein blend that is specifically made for healthy turtle growth and each pellet is made for easy feeding.

Overall, most turtle foods we have recommended have high quality that will provide great nutrition for your pet's growth and maintenance of its health. It is up to your preference on the brand that you want to choose. Take up suggestions from your friends and family on the best food to choose.

This section has provided you with enough knowledge regarding your pet turtle's nutrition and feeding. Make sure you thoroughly read each subsection as to give the proper care and health to your pet. We hope you have learned a lot from the information we have given you. Read on to know more about your pet wood turtle.

Chapter Six: Husbandry Requirements for Wood Turtles

Wood Turtles are ectothermic species which means that their own body temperature depends and adapts to the temperature of their environment. Part of good tending for this docile yet exotic species is to ensure that their environment have just the right kind of warm and cool temperature so that they can eat their food, and live healthily. You need to maintain a good and clean environment for your wood turtle. This chapter will provide you with the right temperatures for your pet turtle as well as some housing maintenance tips.

A Happy and Healthy Home

Each breed of turtle requires different yet specific housing requirements to have a healthy and happy lifestyle. Here, we will give you the basic guidelines that you need to provide your pet wood turtle.

Cage or a Terrarium

To have a happy life, your pet wood turtle should have a long and wide aquarium that will enable them to have a lot of room to bask, move around, and swim. If you are building a terrarium for your hatchling, make sure you get an estimate on how big your pet will be.

An individual turtle needs around 20 gallons of aquarium for itself, if you plan on getting more, add at least 10 gallon per turtle. Add a mesh lid that could provide proper ventilation and UVB light penetration.

An ideal aquarium should have two regions: the land and water region. The division of your region could be up to 50%. The water on the water region should be deeper than its carapace, so your pet turtle could swim freely and be fully submerged. Add a filter to make sure that your water is always clean.

The land region, on the other hand, is used for basking. You can use soil, sand, or aquarium gravel. See our previous chapters on the best substrate you can give to your pet.

The basking area should have a gentle slope to ensure that your pet turtle could easily climb up the land and into the water; you can create it using a large dock, ramp, smooth rocks, slate, or even driftwood. Again, take into consideration the size of your turtle when creating a basking area. Bigger turtle needs a bigger basking area.

Temperature

Remember the two temperatures needed when creating a great habitat for your pet.

The temperature for the water region should be around 78 degrees Fahrenheit or 25 degrees Celsius. You can manage, maintain, and observe temperature through submersible aquarium heater.

For the land region, also known as the basking area, temperature should be between 80 to 85 degrees Fahrenheit or 26 to 29 degree Celsius. You can set the temperature through heat bulbs placed in basking lamps.

Make sure you always check the temperature of the aquarium through a thermometer to avoid under to overheating. If you set it in improper temperature, it can result to illnesses, lack of appetite, or even death.

Humidity

Humidity is a big factor to create a happy and healthy environment for your pet, make sure you consult your veterinarian for the best humidity for your pet wood turtle.

You could use a hygrometer to monitor the humidity levels. A pro-tip: less humidity is required if you provide your pet with drier substrate such as dry mulch and sand.

Filtration and Cleaning

To maintain a healthy environment, it is an absolute necessity to keep the water clean. If you do not want to have a filter, you need to change the water daily. A filter is a big plus because it will ensure that your turtle will stay sanitary, clean, and safe.

Should you opt to buy a filter, we recommend you to buy a big canister filter, although they might be expensive, they provide great benefits. Canister filters are not easily clogged by the solid wastes produced by your pet wood turtle. They will somehow decrease the work you need to do to maintain a clean environment. However, if you plan to buy an internal filter, please do buy two internal filters, you can produce cleaner and healthier water. Whatever brand or type you buy, make sure you clean and change the filter regularly so it will still be at its best shape.

There are things for you to consider when you are cleaning the water from the water region of your aquarium, first how great your water filter, remember the larger the filter, the better, next the number of your turtle, and how big they are.

Remember, do not overfeed your turtle as it will produce a lot of waste. Lastly, wash your hands before and after washing and cleaning your tank to prevent transmission of diseases.

Landscaping/Aquascaping

Although they do not need many items in their aquarium, you need to provide some items that could make them feel they are safe and mimic the environment they have on their natural habitat. You can add terrestrial plants and logs to create a secure place. Further, you can add aquatic plants in the water region to provide great hiding spots and to maintain clean water for a longer time.

Provide smooth flat rocks, wooden enclosures, or even worn driftwood to have a great hiding spot for your wood turtle. Also, add a combination of artificial and real plants, however if you see that they like to eat it – replace the plants with real plants. Consult your veterinarian with the best type of plant you can place in your aquarium.

Lighting

We can't stress enough that your pet wood turtle needs both UVA and UVB bulbs in their tank. UVA is needed to have and encourage breeding, appetite, and proper activity levels while UVB is needed for the production of Vitamin D3 and can stimulate their natural environment, which could decrease their stress.

Put up a timer to produce natural light cycles. Light should be 12 to 14 hours, while darkness should be 10 to 12 hours. Light periods are longer in the summer and shorter during winter time.

To conclude, here are the things that you need to have to produce a happy and healthy life for your pet.

Basic Housing Checklist:

- ☐ Screen Cover for Fresh Air
- ☐ Dome light
- ☐ Red or Black Reptile Bulb
- ☐ Fluorescent Strip Light equipped with UV bulb
- ☐ Timer
- ☐ Air and Water Thermometer
- ☐ Hygrometer
- ☐ Internal Filter, large enough to accommodate/ fit in your enclosure
- ☐ Submersible Aquarium Heater
- ☐ Land/Basking Areas
  - o Turtle Ramp
  - o Dock
  - o Rocks
  - o Drift Wood
- ☐ Turtle Block

Habitat Tips

- Make sure you give non-chlorinated water to the water region. Natural spring water is the best choice and should be given and available daily for drinking.

- Use a screen cover for fresh air but protect it with mesh as to prevent unwanted particles from dropping in.

- Get UV lights with timers if possible, so you can mimic the light patterns needed by your pet.

- Make sure you have an available thermometer to always check the air and water temperature. (Remember, an imbalance of temperature could eventually lead to death)

- For filters – the bigger the better. Small filters could not hold up the particles it may suck up from terrarium.

- Regulate temperature even in the basking area. Maintain the temperature to only 80 to 85 degrees Fahrenheit. Reduce the air temperature by 10 degrees during nighttime.

- Buy a heating pad to be placed under the tank. This is to maintain water temperature to 70 degrees Fahrenheit.

- Ramp is necessary for the turtle to move from the water region up to the land region (or vice versa)
- Place your terrarium in a place where there is no sudden change of temperature.

- Have a big cage for your pet. Estimate its size and procure a bigger one for its need!

Habitat Maintenance Tips

- Regularly clean and check the terrarium of your pet wood turtle. Make sure there are no wastes, rotten food, and other stuff that would make an unlivable environment for your pet.

- Set specific humidity for your enclosure. Consult a veterinarian on how to set the correct humidity for your pet. Humidity often varies from the substrate that you have used in your enclosure.

- Make sure you check every spot in the enclosure. You would not want to risk the pet of your turtle, further, some disease are transmissible – you could even infect you and your family.

- Remove any uneaten food at least 20 minutes after your turtle has eaten it. Also, regularly change its water for drinking and water from the water region.

- When you clean, make sure to remove the turtle as to clean even under the hiding spots, substrates, and the water region.

- Provide a separate tank if you want to clean the terrarium where the turtle is originally place.

These are some things that you need to consider when you build a happy and healthy habitat for your pet. Keep this in mind as they are vital for the survival for your pet.

Chapter Seven: Handling and Hygiene of Your Wood Turtles

Handling this kind of species, wood turtles, is very easy. Some might even say that they can be compared to a dog due to its tame characteristics. Even if they are still babyish, their sharp claws and powerful bodies could cause you injury, and could also cause them to be stressed if they are not being handled properly.

Improper and sometimes inappropriate handling will make these creatures feel unsafe and uncomfortable, and it could cause potential aggression as well. This chapter will provide you with different techniques on how to properly handle your pet and adjust to its behavior.

Handling and the Hygiene of Your Pet

Just like any other mammals or household pets such as cats, dogs and even snakes, wood turtles should be socialized at a young age. This could be a great way for them to learn to socialize with new people and be relaxed when they have companion with them.

Most wood turtle are great for beginners because they are one of the most docile turtles out there. They can be easily trained and task to learn new tricks.

Handling them actually depends on how domesticated these animals are, so if you acquire a baby Wood Turtle or it was born captive they will be easier to handle and tame since you as the keeper can introduce them the concept of socialization.

Regularly touching them while they are still young will make them get used to you and your scent. You need to set a rule that you are their owner and learn to earn their trust so they could follow your command easily.

Here are some guidelines for you to follow when handling your pet wood turtle:

- Use two hands when you pick up your turtle. Use each hand on each side of the shell, preferable between the back and front legs. It is not a surprise that turtles are good in wiggling out of any situation, some even kick, claw, or even bite.

- Do not try to pick up the turtle using its tail. It can potentially dislocate some bones which is very painful for your pet wood turtle.

- Rotate your turtle head over tail (or tail overhead) rather than doing it side over side when you want to inspect its bottom shell. If you turn your turtle from side to side, it could cause your intestine to twist, which could lead to your pet's death.

- Do not keep your turtle on its back when not necessary. This position is very stressful and unnatural for your pet. When turtles lie on their back, they are vulnerable to predators and feel out of control.

- Put your turtle down as gently as possible. This is to avoid injury to internal organs or its legs.

- Do not hold your turtle if it is still in young age especially on its shell. It can cause permanent damage to its body and shell.
- Do not strike or tap the shell against a hard surface. Also, do not injure the shell as it is a living tissue. This act will be very stressful for your pet.

- Do not move too much when you are holding your turtle. Remember that your pet is a living thing and may suffer from injury and stress when you move it too much. If you must, move smoothly and slowly.

Grooming Your Pet Wood Turtle

Your pet wood turtle and reptiles in general don't need any grooming compared to usual household pets. When it comes to grooming, they pretty much will take care of it by themselves, naturally.

To fully groom your pet wood turtle, you need to always remember to clean your pet wood turtle's tank, if you want your juvenile to grow up to have a happy, long, and healthy life. Make sure you clean your cage at least once a week and change the water daily. Here are some other guidelines for you to follow to fully clean your pet wood turtle's tank:

Water Quality

- Turtles are not as sensitive to water quality as fishes.
- Make sure there are no waste products floating around your water.
- When not cleaned properly, ammonia will form. It is a toxic substance that will irritate your pet wood turtle.
- Make sure to always check water quality.

In this section, we will help you to check the water quality for your pet wood turtle's tank.

It might be scary, at first, that water could potentially kill your pet. You need to be vigilant against all the threats that could potentially harm your pet. If you want to seek professional help, you can always ask your veterinarian about what to do with the water in your pet wood turtle's tank.

Otherwise, you can buy test kits for ammonia. Pet stores usually carry this for those owners who have fishes or reptiles. You can ask for assistance on how to properly use the kits and they could even discuss to you the levels of chemicals in your water.

If the test comes out that the water has a high level of nitrites, nitrates, and ammonia, completely change the water and thoroughly clean it. Scrub in between areas so you can thoroughly check for possible contamination. If the level of ammonia is moderate, make sure you frequently change the waters to avoid it being high.

Here are some tips for you to always maintain a squeaky clean tank for your pet wood turtle:

- Choose a filter that is three to four times the size of your turtle tank.

- It is recommended that you buy a filter with mechanical, chemical, and biological filtration.

- Change your water weekly. This is to prevent bacteria build up.

- Take out parts of your water and replace with fresh ones.

- You can use a siphon or gravel vacuum to remove water from your thank.

- Word of Caution: Do not prime a siphon using your mouth because you might be contaminated by salmonella.

- You can skip adding substrate in your water region.

- Skipping substrate will make it easier to clean and see the wastes and uneaten food.

- You can feed your pet outside in a separate tank.

- Create a separate tank for feeding, this might be an additional task, but you can be assured that there will be no uneaten food floating around the water region.

Other Essential Information

There are still a lot of things that you need to remember when you want to care and groom your pet wood turtle.

First thing you need to know, always wash your hand before and handling your pet wood turtle. This step is required for both you and your pet. You would not want to contract disease from your pet nor transmit disease to it. Remember, prevention is better than cure.

These other information should be taken with caution. Please consult your veterinarian first before doing any other steps. Other pet owners like to trim the beak and nails of their pet wood turtle. Remember, your captive wood turtle has changed environments. They do not have rough roads to keep their beaks and nails trimmed.

The downside of not trimming its nails and beak is that it will develop an overbite. Trimming nails and beak is a two person task, ask assistance from your vet – or if you are experienced enough, ask assistance from your friends.

Nails

Turtle nails tend to overgrow because they do not wear them off too often, especially if you just keep them inside their tank. Clipping your turtle's nail is important as it may get stuck in a carpet of filer, or even might tear the claw with the toe still stuck to it.

Trimming turtle's nails are just the same as other pets. Just do not feed them days before the procedure and make sure you handle them with extreme care.

Beaks

Trimming beaks is a new task for novice pet turtle owners. Since they do not have rough things or dirt to chew on, their beaks will just grow and maintain its length.

You can give your pet wood turtle cuttle fish bone as a chew toy; this will serve as a pre-trimming procedure. On the procedure day, make sure to use a paper fingernail file will not hurt your pet wood turtle.

Here are some steps that you need to take when trimming the beak and nail:

- Do not feed your turtle for a couple of days.

- Take good care when handling your pet turtle. Make sure you have a towel and the necessary materials with you.

- If you are alone, sit down, hold the turtle between your thighs and place them over the towel.

- Make sure you get the turtle to poke its head out. You might need to convince your pet turtle to coax its head out.

- You might need to train your pet wood turtle to have its head touch.
- Hold the turtle's head/hand side by side; never put too much pressure to your pet wood turtle as you may injure it.

- Trim the nails and beak slowly but surely. It might take a while, but make sure your pet turtle is comfortable in this process.

Handling your pet wood turtle is very different from other animals. Take great caution when you are handling them.

Chapter Eight: Breeding and Shipping Wood Turtles

Breeding your pet wood turtle is an essential task to continue its lineage. You need to keep yourself ready with these things as you need to accomplish these things before you start breeding your pet. In this chapter, we will provide you with lots of information, such as breeding basics, setting up breeding condition, incubation, hatching, and egg removal process. Take note of these things as you need to be prepared in this painstaking yet happy process of procreation.

Before you can breed your pet wood turtle, you have to familiarize yourself with your pet, learn more about its biology, its breeding behavior and also ask help from other breeders, veterinarian or attend reptile conferences so that you can have knowledge on how to successfully breed them and become a reputable breeder yourself.

You should not force your pet to breed if you do not want to, remember, you should not aim to breed them to sell rather than breed to continue their lives. Have fun reading and enjoy your journey here.

Sexual Dimorphism

Wood Turtle species are dimorphic animals. You can easily determine their sex through their physical characteristics. Knowledge of their sex is essential to knowing and taking care of their needs in the long run.

How to Set Up the Right Breeding Conditions

The right environmental and feeding conditions will help your wood turtle to procreate. Know the process and prepare for the journey of creating your own pet wood turtle family.

Courtship and mating season start during fall months and occur during afternoon hours (11:00 a.m. – 1:00 p.m.)

For wood turtles, mating is a competitive hierarchy, especially for male. Higher ranked male wood turtle gain more mates rather than its counterpart.

In the wild, male wood turtle would fight to gain access and procreate with its female counterpart. These fights might include aggressive behavior that includes biting or chasing one another, they defend themselves through hiding their heads in their shells.

Higher ranked male would get a higher number of offspring, making them more dominant than other wood turtle. On the other hand, female wood turtle could mate with multiple male and can store multiple sperm from them. Although we do not really know how they store sperm, it has been researched on that they have an internal compartment that could store sperm for a couple of years.

If the female wood turtle has mated with several male, this would ensure fertilization and almost all of the female turtle's egg would be fertilized. Further, this could mean that a female wood turtle could carry offspring from different male wood turtle. But, do not force your female wood turtle to mate with every male turtle it meets. Make sure you provide a safe environment for your female wood turtle for this period.

How to Breed Your Pet Wood Turtle

Breeding occurs during fall months in the afternoon. Make sure you introduce your male and female wood turtle at an early stage so they can socialize with one another.

Male wood turtle will head bob at their female counterpart, if there are other male present in the area – but if not, these aggressive behavior will not be really present.

Female counterpart, on the other hand, may be nipped around their face and neck due to overly anxious male because of copulation attempts, these attempts could go on for several minutes but sometimes last for several long hours. Sometimes, there will be actual bites and injuries.

Copulation could happen anywhere, in their terrestrial region, or even in the aquatic region. It is often remarked that the females drag their mates where they want to copulate.

Egg Removal, Incubation and Hatching of Eggs

After thirty to 50 days of successful copulation, female wood turtle would begin nesting – in the sense of a normal semiaquatic turtle. They will excavate five to seven inches deep of nest in a corner or some shrubbery inside their terrarium. They could dig their nests up to two hours, but, if they are interrupted, they will abandon their site and try again – but now in a different location.

Female wood turtle will pee on their nest to mark their territory and further prevent is collapsing while they are digging it.

Your female pet wood turtle could lay up to 4 clutches of three to 5 eggs per year. The shapes of these eggs are elongated and may measure up to 11 ¼ inches wide and 2 inches long! Unlike other eggs, these wood turtles are considerably dark in color. You can easily tell the gender of your pet wood turtle through its temperature. Male wood turtle would produce cool temperature, while its female counterpart will produce warm temperature.

A hatchling should be cared for just like an adult. This means you also need to provide higher humidity (80%) and give them easy access to clean and shallow water. Also, you need to give them a good amount of calcium and protein more than the adult. You can help this process through buying a full-spectrum lighting to give them proper calcium processing and great vitamin production. You should provide an 80 to 90 percent protein hatchling diet, and add calcium on top of their food two times a week.

Raising Wood Turtles

Hatchlings could be left in your outdoor enclosure but keep them in close supervision. You can also keep them indoors so you can monitor it for its proper development and growth, and other concerns, such as predation will be eliminated. You need to give them the same light as an adult: UVA, UVB, and natural sunlight – so it can get the best and develop into a great wood turtle that you want to achieve.

Make sure that you keep a close eye on your hatchlings as they are in a very critical stage. You need to be very mindful of its surrounding, because they might play and eat and might have illnesses and diseases at an early stage. Further, you need to have it socialized with its parents and siblings. This could ensure that they will be well behaved when faced with other pets and other people.

Life Cycle of a Wood Turtle

Wood turtles takes a very long amount of time to reach sexual maturity and having a low ability to reproduce but has a high adult survival rate. However, these survival rates do not hold true for juveniles and hatchlings.

You need to know that males establish hierarchies, but would not have territories over their female counterpart. Wood turtles would become sexually mature at the ages of 14 to 18. These mating activities would occur in spring and in fall, but they would often mate successfully in any part of the year. However, it was observed that the best time to mate is in December.

Mating would consist of several hours of dancing, which could occur by the edge of its aquatic region. Mates would initiate the mating and would nudge at any parts of its female counterpart, such as on its shell, head, tail, and leg. Their female counterpart would often flee away and would repeat this process until they have decided to really mate.

Once they really know that would really mate, the male would gently bite the female's head to signal he intercourse. After the biting, the male would mount the female and inseminate it. It is estimated that the time of intercourse would last from 22 to 33 minutes. The copulation would actually happen in water, between the depths of 0.1 and 1.2 meters. But, that will not stop them to copulate on land. During the two mating seasons, the females can be mounted from one to eight times, and most of these would cause successful impregnation.

Nesting often occurs during May and lasts until July. The areas where female would nest needs to receive enough sunlight, soft soil, free from flooding, and are stable enough to hold eggs. During its life, the wood turtle would grow very fast for the first couple of years.

Five years after it is born, it will measure up to 11.5 centimeter (4.5 inches). At this stage, your pet wood turtle is still a juvenile; you need to be careful in handling and taking care of it. They need to start socializing to get to know their new environment.

When it reaches the age of 16, it will reach 16.5 to 17 cm (6.5 to 6.7 in.) that well depends on gender. At this point, they become adults. They need to be trained with new house rules so they can get accustomed to it. Starting early will create a great discipline for your pet.

A captive wood turtle could live up to fifty eight years, while in wild it could live up to forty years. These are the essential information of the life cycle of your beloved wood turtle. It is a long time commitment, but you will surely enjoy the process as these breed is pretty docile and easy to take care.

How to Package Your Wood Turtles

The packaging is very important if you're going to ship baby wood turtles because you need to make sure that the animals are well protected. You can partner up with other businesses that shipped reptiles so that you can get the lowest rate possible.

Step #1: Prepare a box or a normal size cube that measures around 10 x 10 inches. Make sure that the box is quite thick and made up of quality cardboards.

Step #2: Don't forget to print out a sign that says "perishable goods" or "handle with care" and put some arrows in it in red font color so that the delivery man will take care of it during delivery.

Step #3: Cut out or buy a Styrofoam that's the same size and shape of your box. The foam inserts has two functions, the first one is that they cushion the package inside and the second one is it insulates the animal from outside temperatures, so that you or your customers won't have to worry about the turtles getting too cold or whatnot. Just slide the foams on all sides of the box, make sure that they're exactly fitted in the box's size.

Step #4: Buy plastic cups that look like a water dish or sort of a shallow bowl (not the glass cups,). Once you do, just go ahead and put air holes in it using a tool to poke through the cup.

Step #5: Make a couple of air holes on the plastic cup but not on the box or the foam otherwise it will defeat the purpose of the foam's insulation capabilities because it will let the outside air get inside the box and could make your turtles uncomfortable during its shipment. You can assure your customers by explaining to them that unlike mammals or humans, turtles don't breathe as much as we do since they are cold – blooded creatures, so they won't have to worry about the animal not getting enough air inside the box or becoming suffocated because the foams are not air tight, it's only insulated.

Step #6: Prepare your turtle's bedding. Just tear out a newspaper and crumple it, then put it inside the cup because it will serve as the temporary bedding of the baby turtles. After doing that, you can go ahead and pick out which baby turtle is going to go.

Step #7: Make sure that the turtles are responsive. Check if the turtle has bright and clear eyes, and free of any discharge. Behaviorally speaking, they should be quite scared when getting picked up since they're still babies, they could sort of pull back into their shells – that's actually a good sign that you've properly nursed them.

Step #8: Make sure that the turtles are also soaked or hydrated before packing them up because you just never know how long the shipment could take or whatnot, this is just to prepare them for a trip before reaching their new homes. Usually, depending on how far you're going to deliver them, these turtles are going to be spending around 2 days or more but you don't have to worry about that since they pretty much naturally stay underground as hatchlings.

Step #9: After checking them, place them inside the cup, put the lid and close it. After that, place the cup inside the box then just take a couple more shreds of newspapers, crumple them up and place it in the four corners with the cup being the center to prevent it from getting swayed on either sides of the box.

Step #10: You can include whatever you want like before you sealed the box, just place some instructions, reminders, a thank you note or some kind of surprise for your customer. Take a couple more crumpled newspapers and put them on top to provide added security. You also have to attach a small packaged size heat pad inside the insulated roof (insert it inside the box before completely closing it) to keep the turtle warm as well. Once it's all done, just insert the top piece of foam and close the box using a packaging tape to completely seal it.

The packaging doesn't have to be pretty but it has to be secure. Before shipping a turtle, make sure that you do your research about the particular species because obviously the instructions provided here may only be applicable to wood turtles. Try to also read or research the laws regarding shipping or selling particular turtle species because some breeds could be prohibited in being delivered.

Chapter Nine: Common Diseases and Treatments

Wood Turtles in general might look like an animal that could never get sick, because they do not look like healthy creature every day. They're born in the wild; their mothers left them at an early age, they survive on their own even when they were just hatchlings, they know how to hunt for their own food, and most of the time if they encounter a predator they usually isn't scared of it because that's how confident they are with themselves.

Although they might seem strong at first sight, we must really keep an open eye and see if our pet wood turtle is really healthy. You might not know that they are not hurting inside although they might seem fine inside.

Here, we will list down several illnesses and common diseases that a wood turtle would have. Read on and know how to deal with these things, you might not know your pet wood turtle might need help.

Superficial Wounds

Superficial wounds are very common in wood turtles and turtles in general. Scratches and cuts might happen often especially if you have a big number of turtle in your area.

You do not need to worry about these superficial wounds and you should rush your pet to the vet immediately. What you need to do, as a great wood turtle owner, is to treat the wound immediately because if it gets infected – it will get worse and will cost you a lot of money.

You can use disinfectant, bandage, and a typical triple antibiotic ointment. Clean the scratch or cut with a turtle – proof disinfectant and inspect the wounded part. Remove the debris such as sand or gravel. Finally, put a bandage for it heal quicker. Set aside your turtle in a safe area for the flies to avoid laying eggs within the vicinity of the wound, and clean the injured part daily until it is fully healed.

Respiratory Infection

Respiratory infection is a common illness that will affect your turtle. Some symptoms or observable signs include:

- Lack of energy
- Swollen eyes
- Discharge
- Sneezing
- Trouble breathing
- Wheezing
- Stop eating
- Runny nose
- Bubbles coming from nose or its eyes
- Open mouth breathing
- Raspy breathing

Some causes of lung illnesses will include several viruses and bugs such as Mycoplasma Agassizii and Runny Nose Syndrome (RNS). There is also fungal and viral virus that would cause these illnesses. This will occur if the living condition is too cold or too damp.

Metabolic Bone Disease (MBD)

Metabolic Bone Disease is a result from improper calcium metabolism. The main effect of this can be seen from the bones of the body; your pet might be crippling, or worse, could even die from this disease.

Other terms for this MBD are as follows: osteoporosis, rickets, fibrous osteodystrophy, secondary nutritional hyperparathyroidism, and osteomalacia.

Causes of MBD are the following:

- High levels of phosphorus
- Low or high levels of Vitamin D3 (Must be maintained on the balanced level)
- Inadequate amount of protein
- Insufficient UVA and UVB.
- Poor environmental condition (too cool or too hot)
- High presence of oxalates and fats in the diet, which can result to low calcium absorption.

To avoid this, you need to find the best turtle food you can give to your wood turtle. Or, find supplements that would supply enough vitamin D3 and calcium for your pet.

Diarrhea

A diarrhea episode is a sign there's something wrong with your pet turtle. The common color of the turtle's feces should be firm, must be darkish in color, and should have little to no odor. Some main causes of diarrhea will include: eating watery food like fruits, low fiber diet, internal parasites.

What you need to do is set aside your pet and quarantine it in a separate tank so you can fully monitor it, make changes related to these things, if nothing changes, rush your pet immediately to the vet.

Dehydration

You might think that dehydration is a common thing for your wood turtle, but your pet needs an adequate source of water.

Eye Problem

Your turtle's eyes should be clear, shiny, open, and free from all debris. You need to check its eyes so you can fight off any illnesses and infection. If you have observed that an eye or both eyes are crusty, has pus (or a cheesy – like substance) under the eyelids, swollen, sunken, or have problem opening them – this is a good sign that something is wrong with your eye.

If your turtle has problem seeing, it will not probably eat which could lead to more complication. You need to know the underlying issue to treat the eye problem easily.

Sometimes, eye problems are just a result of improper humidity levels, respiratory infection, or poor hydration. You need to see if there is small debris stuck in its eye. Also, check to see if the substrate pokes their eyes, or if the filter contains debris that potentially spit out debris in the air.

Abscesses

Bumps, lumps, or swelling under the skin of your pet wood turtle are symptoms of the formation of abscesses. These could appear at any part of your pet wood turtle's body. They are very prone to a middle ear infection, which often results to aural abscess which can be seen on the side of their heads.

Other causes include: respiratory illness, or poor care for the turtle terrarium because of contaminated water, too cold temperature, too high or too low humidity levels, and improper nutrition or diet. Most of these circumstances will breed bacteria and infect one's body.

If it is your first time treating an abscess, you need to take your pet immediately to the vet. Ask assistance from the vet and learn how to clean and drain the pus yourself.

Shell Rot

Septemic Cutaneous Ulcerative Disease (SCUD) or shell rot is caused when an open wound or a scratch connected with some injury is further infected with an opportunistic pathogen such as a fungal or bacterial infection.

A wet rot and fungal infection causes a white rot that is rooted from bacterial infection. This kind of infection can only occur in aquatic species, but can also happen with wood turtles. You can easily spot a wet rot due to its discolored shell, and a smell that may or may not be rotten. Further symptoms include pitted, flaky and whitish patches on the shell.

These are some of the diseases and illnesses that would come in the way of your beloved wood turtle. You should know these thing as they might occur not just only once, but recurrent in their lifetime. Keep these in mind as they could potentially lead to death of your beloved pet wood turtle.

Chapter Ten: Care Sheet and Summary

Now that you have learned enough knowledge about Wood Turtle, it is now time for your acquire your Wood Turtle and take your knowledge into action! There are still other references that you can read, such as books, encyclopedia, and websites, that could further enrich your knowledge in wood turtle. This will enable you to become the best pet owner that has the happiest and healthiest pet.

This last part will give you the overview of our beloved friend. Take note of these things as they might come handy someday.

Basic Wood Turtle Information

Taxonomy: Kingdom Animalia, Phylum Chordata, Reptilia Class, Testudines Order, Emydidae Family, Emydinae Subfamily, Glyptemys Genus, G. Insculpta Specie

Distribution and Range: scattered among United States and Canada: Maine, Delaware, New York, Maryland, Massachusetts, Michigan, Iowa, Vermont, New Brunswick, Connecticut, Quebec, Rhode Island, Pennsylvania, New Hampshire, Virginia, West Virginia, Rhode Island, Nova Scotia, and Ontario.

Breed Size: Medium size

Body Type and Appearance: lower shell is yellow with big black blotches on each segment. The top and rear leg portions can be black, brown, or gray. There is a yellowish and orange shade on the skin between the scales, throat, and leg sockets.

Length: average of fourteen to 20 centimeters, some might go up to 211 millimeters. Male reaches up to 23.4 cm while female reaches up to 20.4 cm.

Height: seven to nine inches

Weight: an adult turtle could weigh as heavy as a kilo

Skin Texture: the texture is rough, sculpted shell

Color: Have a black and yellow pattern with dark patches and several yellowish spots. There are variations in the vibrancy of colors

Temperament: alert, inquisitive, responsive, "dog-like"

Diet: opportunistic eaters who are also omnivores; eats a variety of plant material such as various berries, leaves, and mushrooms, mollusks, young mice, amphibians, carrion, earthworms, insects

Habitat: prefers both terrestrial and aquatic habitat; needs small to fast moving streams, terrestrial habitat is required for nesting purposes. They tend to live in deciduous and coniferous forests.

Health Condition: gets along well with other pets

Behavior: In Spring, they are in vegetation. In summer, they are on terrestrial grounds. In winter, they stay under the water.

Life Span: forty years in the wild, while fifty eight years in captivity

Wood Turtles as Pets

Temperament: They tend to move from terrestrial and aquatic area; male wood turtles are very aggressive; they capture their prey easily through stumping their feet imitating the sound of the rainfall; they are docile creatures; they are shy; if they are trained in a proper environment, they can become excellent pets; they spend time foraging for food; they bask; they rarely venture away from the place they were born, in its entire life; intelligent; it can live in streams, creeks, woods, thickets, meadows, rivers, and swamps; they hibernate in winter; they are quite agile.

Major Pro: They are very easy to manage especially for novice pet owners. They can eat pretty much everything since they are omnivores and opportunistic feeders. You will have a breeze in taking care of them.

Major Con: It lives up to forty eight to fifty years which means you need to have a long term commitment. Further, you need to have a terrarium of different regions to ensure that your pet will have different temperatures at all times.

Legal Requirements and Wood Turtle Licensing:

- Wood Turtles are specifically not threatened of extinction, but its trade should be control to avoid extinction or even using it beyond its capacity to survive.

- You will not be able to travel with your Wood Turtle from one country to another one if you do not have necessary certificates proving that you can move it from one place to another.

- Keep necessary documents close as it may be needed whenever you travel with your pet wood turtle.

- Wood turtle trade is controlled; buy from licensed people or pet store.

Estimated Costs of Keeping a Wood turtle:

- Water Dish: $20 or more
- Wood Turtle breed: $320-$400
- Glass Enclosure with a screen top or lid: average of $99
- Glass Enclosure (for adults): $250 (complete set with regulators/heaters)
- Substrate: $6/bag
- Heaters/Misting Equipment: around $40 total or more
- Basking Lamp/UVB bulbs: $100 or more
- Heat and Water Temperature Regulator/ Gauges: $5 or more
- Food: $12/bag or more (depending on brand and amount/quantity)

How to Acquire a Wood Turtle

Where to Purchase: Reptile Shops, Private Breeders, Reptile Shows, Rescue Centers

Characteristics of a Reputable Breeder:

- They should be able to teach you how to properly set up the enclosure, where to place it, and the right temperature/humidity levels needed.

- Good breeders will walk you through every step of the process. They are willing to answer all of your questions and if they think that you are not a good fit as an owner, they won't sell it to you.

- Good breeders must be knowledgeable about the breeds they raise, and should give you specific info about the breed.

Characteristics of a Healthy Breed:

- Make sure that its eyes are free from any cloudiness or discharge.
- make sure that your pet wood turtle is not having a hard time breathing
- There no discharge from the nose.

- the wood turtle must be mobile
- Can move at its will.

Setting Up a Habitat for Wood Turtle

- Ideally, the temporary cage for a baby wood turtle should be a 55 – gallon tank, and once it becomes an adult the cage size should at least be 6 feet in length, 3 to 4 feet in height and 4 to 6 feet in depth.
- You need to make sure that the enclosure you will buy or build is either made out of thick glass/plexiglass or thick plywood because these animals have very sharp claws that can easily rip the enclosure apart if it's made out of mesh or low quality materials.
- Don't want to buy very large materials to put inside a cage if the enclosure itself doesn't have a wide opening or somewhat hard to access. You can also opt to purchase a glass tank since it's much affordable and provides an accessible sliding doors or glass lids.

Materials Needed for Wood Turtle Enclosure:

- Substrate
- Water Dishes
- Hiding Spots
- UVB light
- Heaters
- Basking light bulbs

Diet for Wood turtles

In the wild: wood turtles like eating earthworm as well as slugs, leeches, snails, larvae, frogs, newborn mice, tadpoles. They can also eat plants, algae, grasses, leaves of willow, birch, alder and even cranberry leaves.

In Captivity: You can give the following food to your turtles:

- Strawberries
- Raspberries
- Apple
- Bananas
- Cherries
- Pear
- Grapes
- Watermelon

- Cantaloupe
- Honeydew melon
- Carrots
- Mixed vegetables (purchased at supermarket)
- Spinach
- Romaine lettuce
- Corn
- Minnows
- Canned dog food
- Earthworms
- Adult live crickets
- Kitten chow
- Hard-boiled egg
- Dead mice
- Chicken heart and liver

Feeding Amount/Frequency:

- Juveniles need to eat daily because they need vitamins and minerals in their system.
- When they reach the age of seven, or if they stop eating regularly, you can opt to feed it every other day or every three days.

Husbandry for Wood turtle

Lighting, Temperature and Humidity Guidelines:

- The temperature for the water region should be around 78 degrees Fahrenheit or 25 degrees Celsius.
- For the land region, also known as the basking area, temperature should be between 80 to 85 degrees Fahrenheit or 26 to 29 degree Celsius.
- You can set the temperature through heat bulbs placed in basking lamps.
- Add the necessary UVA and UVB lights needed by your wood turtle.
- Consult your veterinarian on how to properly set the humidity in the tank.

Habitat Maintenance Tips:

- Clean and check the terrarium of your pet wood turtle.
- There should be no wastes, rotten food, and other stuff that would make a nasty environment for your pet.

- Make sure you check every spot in the enclosure. You would not want to risk the pet of your turtle, further, some disease are transmissible – you could even infect you and your family.

- Remove any uneaten food at least 20 minutes after your turtle has eaten it. Also, regularly change its water for drinking and water from the water region.

- When you clean, make sure to remove the turtle as to clean even under the hiding spots, substrates, and the water region.

Handling Tips:

- Use two hands when you pick up your turtle.
- Do not try to pick up the turtle using its tail.
- Do not keep your turtle on its back when not necessary. This position is very stressful and unnatural for your pet. When turtles lie on their back, they are vulnerable to predators and feel out of control.
- Put your turtle down as gently as possible. This is to avoid injury to internal organs or its legs.

- Do not hold your turtle if it is still in young age especially on its shell. It can cause permanent damage to its body and shell.
- Do not strike or tap the shell against a hard surface. Also, do not injure the shell as it is a living tissue. This act will be very stressful for your pet.
- Do not move too much when you are holding your turtle. Remember that your pet is a living thing and may suffer from injury and stress when you move it too much. If you must, move smoothly and slowly.

Breeding Your Wood turtles

How to Set Up the Right Breeding Conditions:

- Courtship and mating season start during fall months and occur during afternoon hours (11:00 a.m. – 1:00 p.m.)
- For wood turtles, mating is a competitive hierarchy, especially for male. Higher ranked male wood turtle gain more mates rather than its counterpart.
- Higher ranked male would get a higher number of offspring, making them more dominant than other wood turtle.

Common Diseases and Health Requirements

- Generally, healthy but predispose to Intestinal Parasites, Fatty Liver Disease, Metabolic Bone Disease (MBD), Bacterial Pneumonia

- Superficial Wounds
- Respiratory Infections
- Diarrhea
- Doesn't Poop
- Dehydrated
- Eye Problems
- Abscesses
- Accidental Drowning
- Overgrown Claws/Beak
- Won't Eat
- Deformed Shell
- Cracked Shell
- Shell Rot
- Mouth Rot
- Pregnancy Issues
- Paralyzed Limbs
- Internal Parasites
- External Parasites
- Mites and Ticks
- Blowfly Botfly
- Gout

Viral Infections

- After you have read all of these things, you now have the basic information about your desired pet – the wood turtle. These majestic creatures is very much suited for you, you need to keep an open mind, open heart, and open soul to fully connect with your pet now.

Glossary

Acclimation – Adjusting to a new environment or new
conditions over a period of time

Acrylic Aquarium – Glass aquarium alternative, usually
lighter than an ordinary aquarium but can be easily
scratched.

Active range – The area of activity which can include
hunting, seeking refuge, and finding a mate

Ambient temperature – The overall temperature of the
environment

Amelanistic – Amel for short; without melanin, or without any black or brown coloration.

Ammonia – made up of nitrogen and hydrogen. It has an unpleasant smell that's also toxic and corrosive. Leftover food in the enclosure can be contributing factors that build up ammonia

Anerythristic – Anery for short; without any red coloration.

Aquatic – Lives in water.

Arboreal – Lives in trees.

Bacteria – microorganisms that are distributed widely in the environments. Turtle keepers should be aware of the harmful effects of bacteria
Bacteria Bloom – sometimes referred to as a tank syndrome.

Basking – a procedure where tortoises or turtles warms or dries up their body. Tortoises/turtles will need to have a basking area at a certain temperature to prevent shell rot. It also allows absorption of UVA and UVB for thermoregulation
Betadine – An antiseptic that can be used to clean wounds in reptiles

Bilateral – Where stripes, spots or markings are present on both sides of an animal.

Biotic – The living components of an environment.

Bridge – part of the shell that's located in the middle of the front and black legs connecting the top and bottom shell.

Brumation – The equivalent of mammalian hibernation among reptiles

Cannibalistic – Where an animal feeds on others of its own kind.

Cloaca – also vent; a half-moon shaped opening for digestive waste disposal and sexual organs.

Cloacal Gaping – Indication of sexual receptivity of the female.

Cloacal Gland – A gland at the base of the tail which emits foul smelling liquid as a defense mechanism; also called Anal Gland.

Clutch – A batch of eggs.

Constriction – The act of wrapping or coiling around a prey to subdue and kill it prior to eating.

Crepuscular – Active at twilight, usually from dusk to dawn.

Diurnal – Active by day

Drop – To lay eggs or to bear live young

Ectothermic – Cold-blooded. An animal that cannot regulate its own body temperature, but sources body heat from the surroundings

Endemic – Indigenous to a specific region or area.

Estivation – Also Aestivation; a period of dormancy that usually occurs during the hot or dry seasons in order to escape the heat or to remain hydrated.

Flexarium – A reptile enclosure that is mostly made from mesh screening, for species that require plenty of ventilation.

Fossorial – A burrowing species.

Gestation – The period of development of an embryo within a female.

Gravid – The equivalent of pregnant in reptiles

Gut-loading – Feeding insects within 24 hours to a prey before they are fed to your pet, so that they pass on the nutritional benefits

Hatchling – A newly hatched, or baby, reptile.

Herps/Herpetiles – A collective name for reptile and amphibian species.

Herpetoculturist – A person who keeps and breeds reptiles in captivity

Herpetologist – A person who studies ectothermic animals, sometimes also used for those who keeps reptiles.

Herpetology – The study of reptiles and amphibians.

Hide Box – A furnishing within a reptile cage that gives the animal a secure place to hide.

Husbandry – The daily care of a pet reptile.

Hygrometer – Used to measure humidity.

Impaction – A blockage in the digestive tract due to the swallowing of an object that cannot be digested or broken down.

Incubate – Maintaining eggs in conditions favorable for development and hatching.

Juvenile – Not yet adult; not of breedable age

LTC – Long Term Captive; or one that has been in captivity for more than six months.

MBD – Metabolic Bone Disease; occurs when reptiles lack sufficient calcium in their diet.

Morph – Color pattern

Musking – Secretion of a foul smelling liquid from its vent as a defense mechanism.

Oviparous – Egg-bearing.

Ovoviviparous – Eggs are retained inside the female's body until they hatch.

Popping – The process by which the sex is determined among hatchlings.

Probing – The process by which the sex is determined among adults.

Sloughing – Shedding.

Sub-adult – Juvenile

Substrate – The material lining the bottom of a reptile enclosure.

Stat – Short for Thermostat

Tag – Slang for a bite or being bitten

Terrarium – A reptile enclosure.

Thermo-regulation – The process by which cold-blooded animals regulate their body temperature by moving from hot to cold surroundings.

Vent – Cloaca

Vivarium – Glass-fronted enclosure

Viviparous – Gives birth to live young.

WC – Wild Caught

WF – Wild Farmed; refers to the collection of a pregnant female whose eggs or young were hatched or born in captivity.

Yearling – A year old.

Zoonosis – A disease that can be passed from animal to man.

Photo Credits

Page 1 Photo by user big4stage2screen via Pixabay.com, https://pixabay.com/en/turtle-woods-natural-forest-2923006/

Page 4 Photo by user John Brandauer via Flickr.com,

Page 99 Photo by user Tom Murray via Flickr.com,
https://www.flickr.com/photos/tmurray74/36799838936/

References

"American Wood Turtle Species" - PSU.edu

http://www.psu.edu/dept/nkbiology/naturetrail/speciespage
s/woodturtle.htm

"Care Sheet for Turtles "- RepticZone.com

http://www.repticzone.com/caresheets/209.html

"Captive Care And Breeding Of The Central American Ornate Wood Turtle" – ReptilesMagazine.com

http://www.reptilesmagazine.com/Turtles-Tortoises/Turtle-Care/Central-American-Ornate-Wood-Turtle/

"How to Care for American Wood Turtles (with Notes on Natural History)" – That Reptile Blog

http://blogs.thatpetplace.com/thatreptileblog/2013/04/04/how-to-care-for-american-wood-turtles-with-notes-on-natural-history/#.WkOJwfCWbIU

"Keeping Turtles as Pets" – Pets4Homes.co.uk

https://www.pets4homes.co.uk/pet-advice/keeping-turtles-as-pets.html

"Ornate Wood Turtles: Rhinoclemmys Pulcherrima manni" - Ectotherms.net

http://ectotherms.net/kyherpsoc/woodturtlecare.htm

"North American Wood Turtle" – PetGuide.com

http://www.petguide.com/breeds/turtle/north-american-wood-turtle/

"Pet Turtles: Ornate Wood Turtle Care and Breeding" – That Reptile Blog http://blogs.thatpetplace.com/thatreptileblog/2014/07/17/pet-turtles-ornate-wood-turtle-care-and-breeding/#.WkONJfCWbIU

"The Beginners Guide to Keeping Terrapins & Turtles" PBS Pet Travel UK

https://www.pbspettravel.co.uk/blog/the-beginners-guide-to-keeping-terrapins-turtles/

"Turtle Care 101: How to Take Care of Pet Turtles" – Petmd.com

https://www.petmd.com/reptile/care/evr_rp_how-to-take-care-of-pet-turtles

"Turtle Care Guide" – VetBabble.com

https://www.vetbabble.com/reptiles/turtles/

"Wood Turtle: Glyptemys Insculpta" – CT. gov

http://www.ct.gov/deep/cwp/view.asp?a=2723&q=475304

"Wood Turtle" - Allturtles.com

https://www.allturtles.com/wood-turtle/

"Wood Turtle" - Wikipedia.org

https://en.wikipedia.org/wiki/Wood_turtle

"Wood Turtle Diet" – WoodTurtle.com

http://www.woodturtle.com/Diet.html

Made in the USA
Monee, IL
09 September 2021